Being a Scientist

Young learners need to know that scientists are not just workers wearing white jackets in laboratories. We do science when we

- cook breakfast
- mix paints to make new colors
- plant seeds in the garden
- watch a squirrel in a tree
- mark how tall we are on a growth chart, or
- look outside to see what the weather is like

The scientists in the science laboratories and those in the kindergarten or first-grade classroom use important science processes to do their work. This book helps students to recognize and experience those processes.

The activities in this book relate to the National Science Education Standards (Science as Inquiry). When you follow the step-by-step lessons, your students will be doing science. They will

- observe
- predict
- compare
- order
- categorize
- ask meaningful questions
- conduct investigations
- record information
- communicate investigations and explanations
- use tools and equipment

What makes this book easy for you?

- The step-by-step activities are easy to understand and include illustrations where it's important.
- The resources you need are at your fingertips: record sheets; logbook sheets; and other reproducibles such as minibooks, task cards, and picture cards.
- Each science concept is presented in a self-contained section. You can decide to do the entire book or pick only those sections that enhance your own curriculum.

minibooks

task cards

logbooks

picture cards

Using Logbooks as Learning Tools

ScienceWorks for Kids emphasizes the use of logbooks to help students summarize and solidify learning.

Logbooks are valuable learning tools for several reasons:

• Logbooks give students an opportunity to put what they are learning into their own words.

• Putting ideas into words is an important step in internalizing new information. Whether spoken or written, this experience allows students to synthesize their thinking.

• Explaining and describing experiences helps students make connections between several concepts and ideas.

• Logbook entries allow the teacher to catch misunderstandings right away and then reteach.

• Logbooks are a useful reference for students and a record of what has been learned.

Two Types of Logbooks

This picture stands for class logbook

As discussions and investigations in this book are completed, the teacher will record student understandings in a class logbook. Even though your students may not be reading, the responses can be read to them as a means of confirming and reviewing learning.

Record student responses on large sheets of chart paper. Pictures drawn by students can be added to illustrate what has been recorded. Use metal rings to hold the pages together.

This picture stands for student logbook

Students process their understanding of investigations by writing or drawing their own responses in individual student logbooks. Following the investigations are record and activity sheets that can be added to each student's logbook.

At the conclusion of the unit, reproduce a copy of the logbook cover on page 3 for each student. Students organize their pages and staple them with the cover.

page 3

Plants

My Logbook

Name:

Teacher Preparation

Note: Caution students about touching or eating plant parts with which they are unfamiliar. If you plan to do tasting of plant parts such as seeds, leaves, etc., check with parents about any allergies students might have.

Plants for Observation

Before beginning this unit on plants, plan opportunities for students to observe plants.

• Have several different types of potted plants in the classroom.

• Take field trips to:

    a neighborhood garden
    a nursery
    a farm or an orchard

• Invite a gardener or farmer to share plants and information with the class.

Clipboards

Make a class set of "clipboards" for students to use when doing observations outside the classroom.

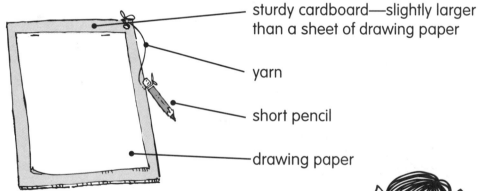

sturdy cardboard—slightly larger than a sheet of drawing paper

yarn

short pencil

drawing paper

Plants for Investigations

Several investigations in this unit require a number of identical small plants. These may be purchased in flats at a nursery, or grown from seeds if you have time.

A Plant Library

Gather an assortment of books about plants. (See the inside back cover for a bibliography to use throughout the study of plants.)

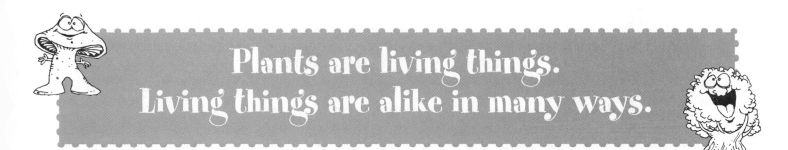

Plants are living things.
Living things are alike in many ways.

Plants Are Living Things

- Display a living plant. Ask students to describe it. Use questioning to encourage responses beyond the plant's appearance.

The plant is green. It can grow big. It has leaves. It is going to have flowers.

Say, "Some of you said that the plant can grow. What do we call things that can grow?" (You may need to use questioning to help students come up with the answer that they are living things.) Ask, "Can you name other living things?"

Living Things
(tree)
(flower)
cat
bug

- List student ideas on chart paper entitled "Living Things." This will be the first page of a class plant logbook. Don't write information not offered by students. Add details as your students acquire more information.

Read each item listed and have students decide if it is a plant or an animal. Circle the plants.

- Refer to plants and animals on the chart and say, "All of the things on this list are living. What can living things do?" The depth of the responses you receive will depend on the prior knowledge of your students.

- Write student responses on a chart entitled "Living things can…." Add the chart to the class logbook.

Living things can...
get bigger
eat
run

Learning About Plants • EMC 868

Is It Living or Nonliving?

- Show something that is nonliving (book, pencil, jacket) and ask questions such as:

  "Can this (name object) grow?"

  "Does it need to eat or drink water?"

  "Is it living?"

  Have students look around the classroom for other nonliving things. List the named items on a chart. Select students to draw pictures of the items for the chart. Paste each picture next to its name.

- Using page 7, students color the plants, circle the animals, and cross out the nonliving things. This will be the first page of the students' logbooks.

- Each student is to draw or paint a picture of a living thing. They then write or dictate a sentence giving one characteristic of something that is alive. Use the pictures to create a bulletin board.

- Using page 8, students draw a plant and an animal, and then answer the "yes/no" questions to show they understand the concept.

Making Connections

Ask, "Are you more like a plant or an animal?" Have students explain their answers. Have students draw themselves, labeling their pictures "I am a living thing."

page 7

page 8

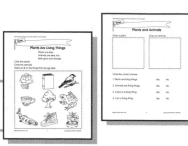

Include these pages in each student's logbook.

Name

Plants Are Living Things

Plants are alive.
Animals are alive, too.
Both grow and change.

Color the plants.
Circle the animals.
Make an **X** on the things that are <u>not</u> alive.

Name

Plants and Animals

Draw a plant.

Draw an animal.

Circle the correct answer.

1. Plants are living things.   Yes   No

2. Animals are living things.   Yes   No

3. A box is a living thing.   Yes   No

4. I am a living thing.   Yes   No

A Plant Hunt

- Divide the class into groups, each with an adult group leader. Each group will need a clipboard, pencil, hand lens, and a copy of the checklist on page 11. Group leaders are to help students identify and record what they observe.

  Send the groups to different areas around the school grounds or other space to see what plants they can find. If possible, make arrangements for students to visit a flower or vegetable garden.

  Note: *Emphasize that nothing is to be touched unless the group leader says it is okay, but do encourage using all the senses where it is appropriate. For example, students might feel the texture of different kinds of bark or the ribs in a leaf; they might smell flowers or leaves of different plants.*

  Back in class, have each group share what they saw. Ask them to describe the different types of plants. "What does a tree look like? How are grass and flowers alike? Are all flowers, trees, or bushes the same?" Use the checklists to tally the types of plants observed. Write the names of the plants on the chart paper, and then, using tally marks, have each group mark off the types of plants they saw.

- Add the tally chart to the class plant logbook.

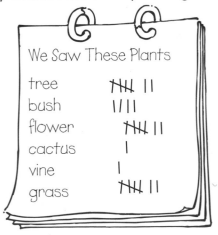

- Using page 12, students color each type of plant they saw, and then draw their favorite plant.

- Sort the cards on pages 13–15 into groups by plant type (tree, flowering plant, bush, etc.). Place the cards in a center for individual student use.

page 11

page 12

pages 13–15

Different Plants in Different Places

- Read the minibook on pages 16–19 to learn more about the different types of plant habitats. Ask students to describe what they see in each environment shown. Help them identify the kinds of plants.

- List several environments on chart paper. Ask students to name some kinds of plants that grow there. Have them refer back to their minibooks for help.

pages 16–19

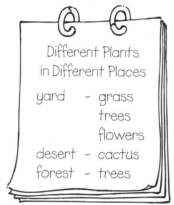

- Show two picture cards from pages 13–15 and ask, "Do these two plants grow in the same kind of place?" Make the differences fairly obvious at this level. Ask students to give at least one reason why the plants would not grow in the same place. *(A cactus grows in the desert and a tree grows in the forest or a field.)*

- Adopt a tree to watch throughout the school year to see seasonal changes. Discuss what is different about the tree at each observation. Have students illustrate the changes.

- Begin class collections of leaves, flowers, or bark rubbings. Place these in a class scrapbook.

Logbook

Include this page in each student's logbook.

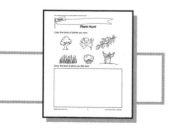

We're Going on a Plant Hunt

Who is in this group?_____

_____

Our group leader is _____

Make a check mark by the types of plants seen on the plant hunt.

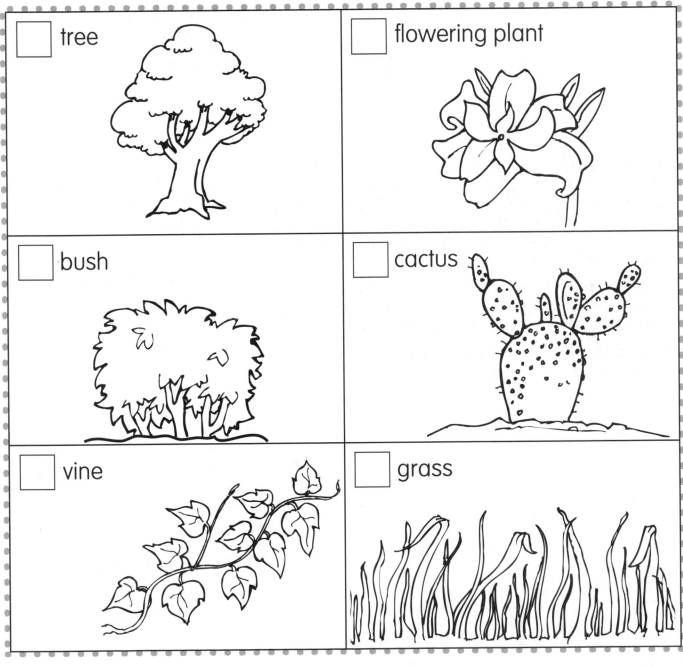

☐ tree	☐ flowering plant
☐ bush	☐ cactus
☐ vine	☐ grass

Learning About Plants • EMC 868

Name

Plant Hunt

Color the kinds of plants you saw.

Draw the kind of plant you like best.

pine tree

©2000 by Evan-Moor Corp. • EMC 868

deciduous tree

©2000 by Evan-Moor Corp. • EMC 868

apple tree

©2000 by Evan-Moor Corp. • EMC 868

bush

©2000 by Evan-Moor Corp. • EMC 868

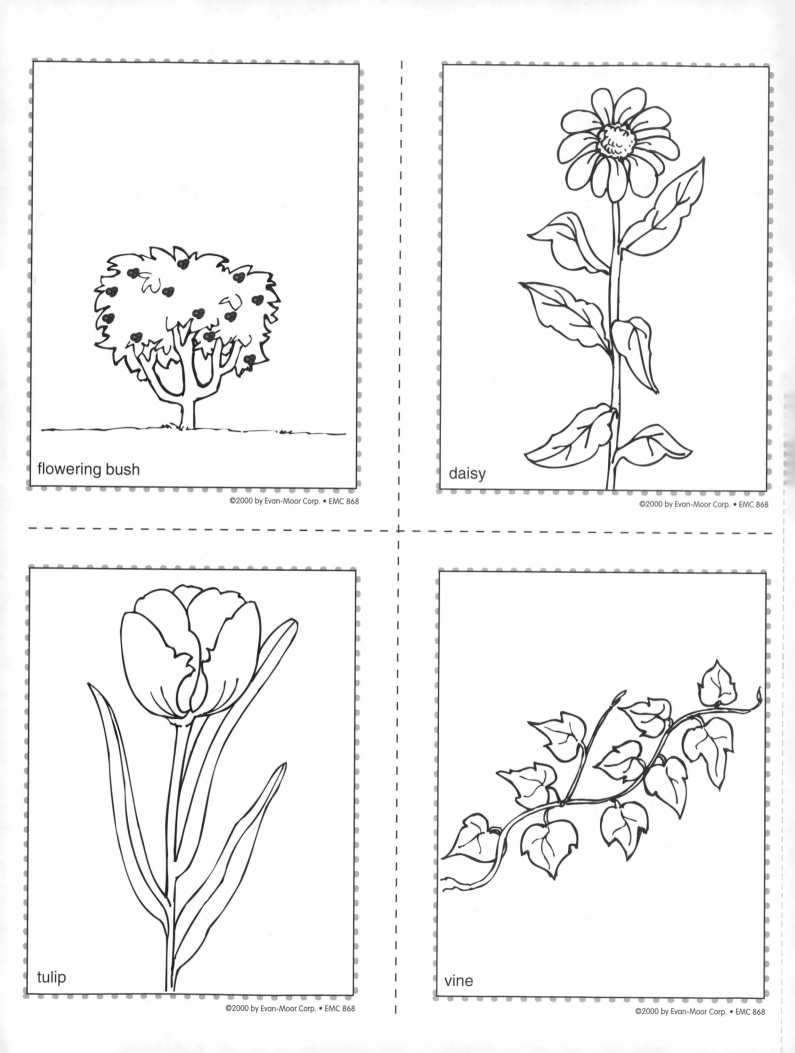

flowering bush

daisy

tulip

vine

saguaro cactus

©2000 by Evan-Moor Corp. • EMC 868

barrel cactus

©2000 by Evan-Moor Corp. • EMC 868

cattail

©2000 by Evan-Moor Corp. • EMC 868

water lily

©2000 by Evan-Moor Corp. • EMC 868

Plants Grow Almost Everywhere

Let's walk around the earth.

Let's see what we can see.

Name:

1

In the rainforest we see…

2

In the redwood
forest we see…

3

In the meadow we see…

4

In a hot desert we see...

5

In a pond we see...

6

In the ocean we see…

7

Learning About Plants • EMC 868

And in our neighborhood we see…

Draw plants in your neighborhood.

8

The parts of a plant help it survive in its environment.

Plants Have Many Parts

- Show one or more plants to your students. Ask them to name what they see. Use questioning, if necessary, until someone gives the word *plants*.

- Ask students to name the parts of the plant. Record their responses on a chart. Additions and corrections can be made as students acquire more information.

  This investigation will help students see the major parts of a flowering plant (roots, stem, leaves, and flowers). Divide the class into small groups or have students work in pairs.

Plant Parts

flower

stem

leaves

roots

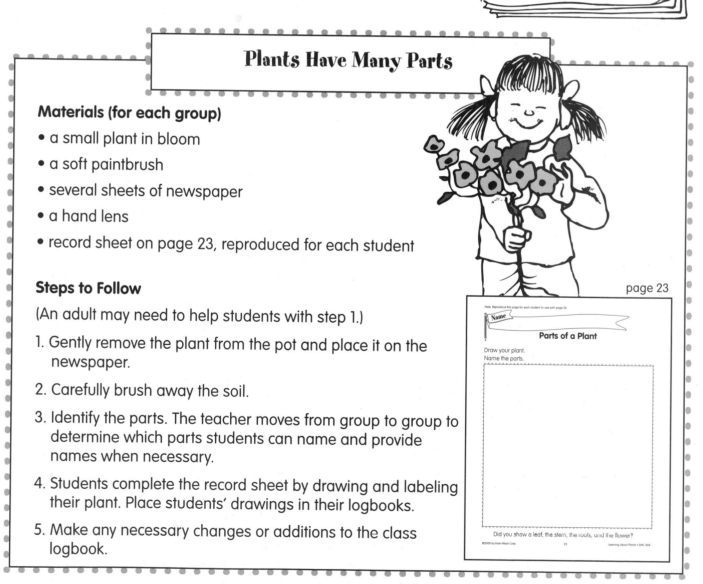

Plants Have Many Parts

Materials (for each group)

- a small plant in bloom
- a soft paintbrush
- several sheets of newspaper
- a hand lens
- record sheet on page 23, reproduced for each student

Steps to Follow

(An adult may need to help students with step 1.)

1. Gently remove the plant from the pot and place it on the newspaper.

2. Carefully brush away the soil.

3. Identify the parts. The teacher moves from group to group to determine which parts students can name and provide names when necessary.

4. Students complete the record sheet by drawing and labeling their plant. Place students' drawings in their logbooks.

5. Make any necessary changes or additions to the class logbook.

page 23

Note: Reproduce this page for each student to use with page 20.

Name

Parts of a Plant

Draw your plant.
Name the parts.

Did you show a leaf, the stem, the roots, and the flower?

©2000 by Evan-Moor Corp.   23   Learning About Plants • EMC 868

Follow-Up

- Make flannel or magnetic board pieces using the patterns on pages 24 and 25.

  Pass out the pieces of a flowering plant to students. Call on the four students to arrange the pieces correctly on the board to create a flowering plant. Repeat the activity with the pieces of a tree.

- Reproduce the folded book on page 26 for each student. Read and discuss the pages together.

- Using page 27, students name the plant parts.

- Show students pictures of two plants (use cards from pages 13–15) that are quite different in appearance (a cactus and a deciduous tree; a vine and a flowering plant; a pine tree and an apple tree). Challenge them to identify the ways in which plants are alike even though they look very different.

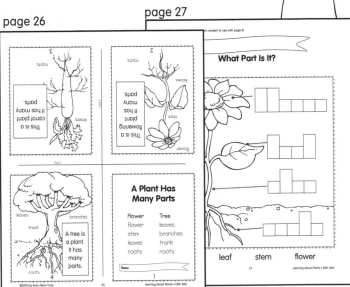

page 26   page 27

Looking at Trees

- Read from books such as *The Tree* by Gallimard Jeunesse and Pascale De Bourgoing and *Crinkleroot's Guide to Knowing the Trees* by Jim Arnosky to introduce a variety of trees to your students. Go outside and look at trees up close. Ask students to name the parts of a tree. Help them identify the roots of the tree and to recognize that the trunk is the tree's stem. Make rubbings of bark patterns. Collect leaves from various kinds of trees.

Place paper against tree bark and rub with the side of a broken crayon.

Collect one leaf from several different trees. Press between sheets of newspaper to dry.

- Back in the classroom, ask students to describe how trees are alike and different from other plants. Record their responses on a chart entitled "Trees" for the class logbook.

- Using page 28, students draw a tree.

page 28

Trees

Trees have leaves.

Some trees are tall.

Include these pages in each student's logbook.

Name

Parts of a Plant

Draw your plant.
Name the parts.

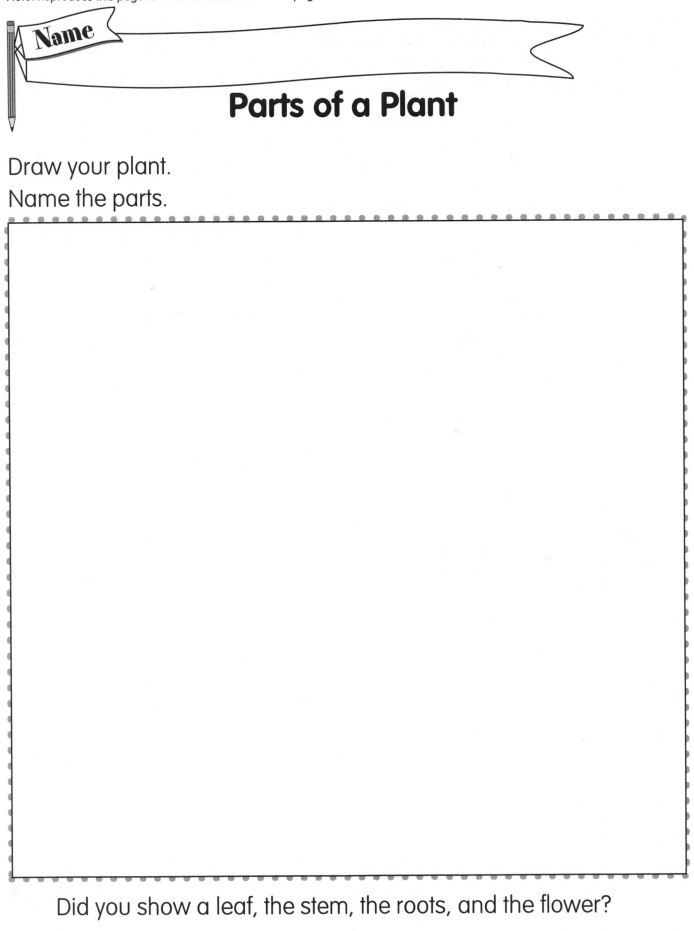

Did you show a leaf, the stem, the roots, and the flower?

 Learning About Plants • EMC 868

Flower Part Patterns

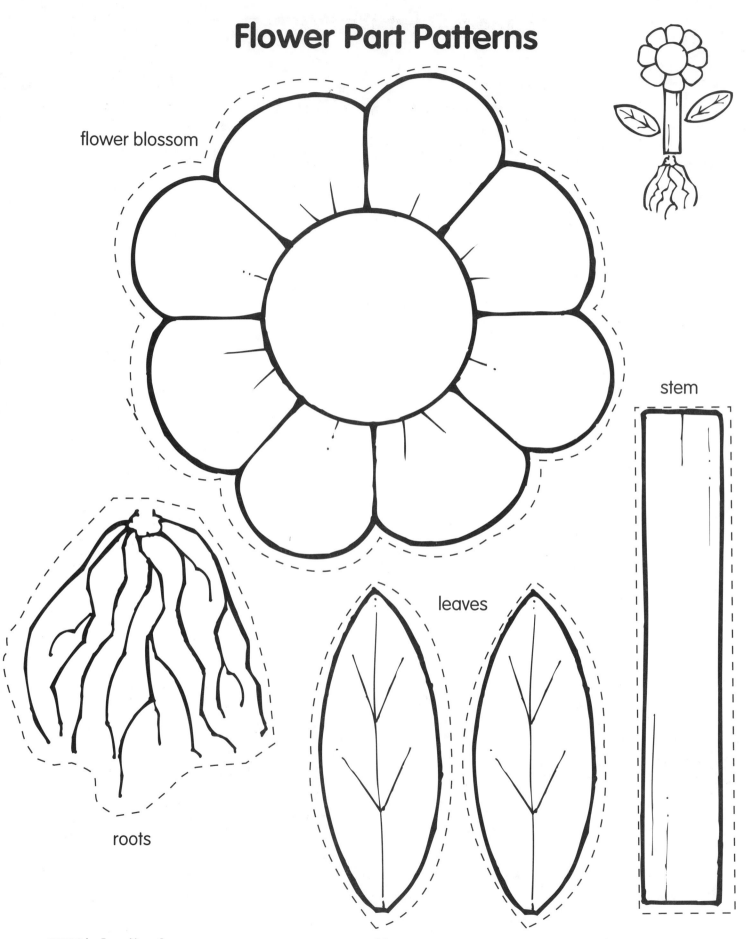

flower blossom

stem

leaves

roots

Learning About Plants • EMC 868

Tree Part Patterns

trunk

branches with leaves

roots

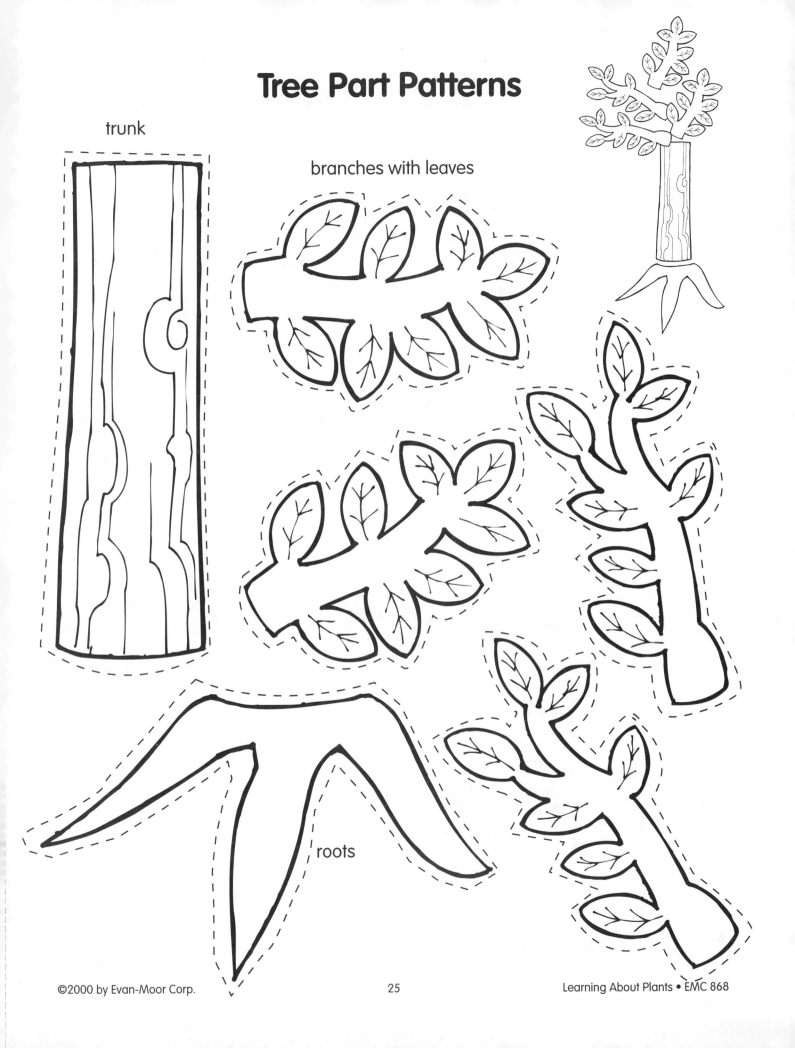

25

Learning About Plants • EMC 868

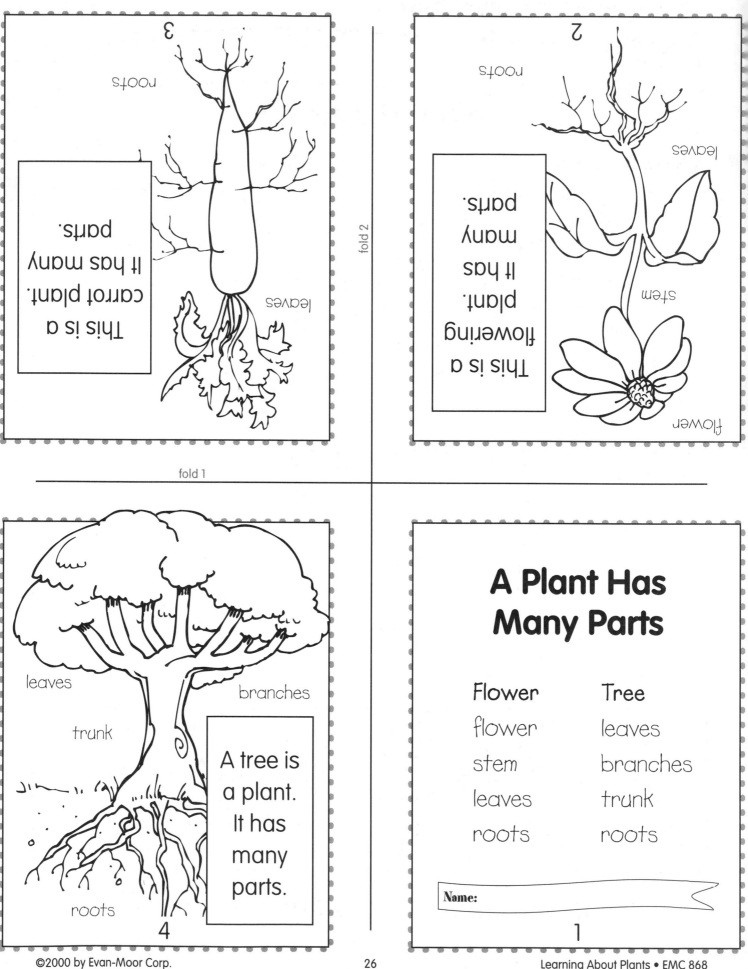

3

roots

This is a carrot plant. It has many parts.

leaves

fold 2

2

roots

leaves

This is a flowering plant. It has many parts.

stem

flower

fold 1

4

leaves

branches

trunk

A tree is a plant. It has many parts.

roots

A Plant Has Many Parts

Flower	Tree
flower	leaves
stem	branches
leaves	trunk
roots	roots

Name:

1

Name

What Part Is It?

Name the parts.

roots   leaf   stem   flower

Learning About Plants • EMC 868

Name

A Tree Is a Plant

A tree has leaves.
A tree has a stem.
A tree has roots.

Draw a tree.

Plants have roots.
Roots collect water.

Plants Have Roots

• Bring in a collection of roots (pull two or three different types of small plants from the soil; bring in carrots, radishes, and a bunch of greens with leaves and roots still attached) to share with students. Ask them to identify and describe the roots of each plant.

• Students draw different types of roots. Paste these to a sheet of chart paper.

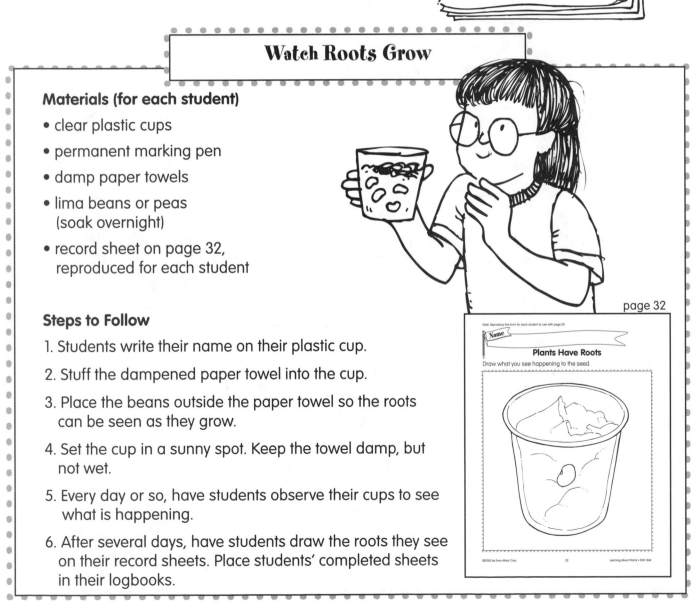

Watch Roots Grow

Materials (for each student)

• clear plastic cups

• permanent marking pen

• damp paper towels

• lima beans or peas (soak overnight)

• record sheet on page 32, reproduced for each student

Steps to Follow

1. Students write their name on their plastic cup.

2. Stuff the dampened paper towel into the cup.

3. Place the beans outside the paper towel so the roots can be seen as they grow.

4. Set the cup in a sunny spot. Keep the towel damp, but not wet.

5. Every day or so, have students observe their cups to see what is happening.

6. After several days, have students draw the roots they see on their record sheets. Place students' completed sheets in their logbooks.

page 32

The Job of Roots

- Ask students to explain what roots do for the plant. Use questioning to help them reach an understanding that roots hold the plant in the soil and they also collect water for the plant.

- Record student responses on a chart.

- Explain to students that this investigation will show them how plant roots collect water for the rest of the plant to use. They are to imagine that the piece of paper towel is a root, and then watch as the water moves up the paper. The investigation can be done as a demonstration, in small groups, or by individual students.

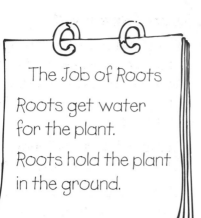

The Job of Roots

Roots get water for the plant.

Roots hold the plant in the ground.

Roots Collect Water

Materials (for each student)

- strips of paper towel 1" x 6" (2.5 cm x 15 cm)
- container of water with red food coloring added
- eyedroppers
- small plastic plates
- record sheet on page 33, reproduced for each student

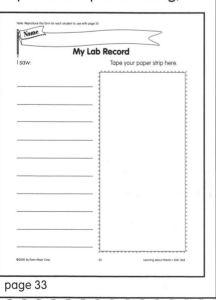

Steps to Follow

1. Ask students to predict what will happen when they put water on one end of their paper strip. Record their predictions on the chalkboard.

2. Students place a paper strip on the plastic plate. They put a drop of water just touching, but not on top of, the paper strip and observe what happens. Repeat the investigation several times to see if the same thing occurs each time.

3. Have students share what they observed. *(The red water moved up the piece of paper towel.)*

    Check to see if everyone has the same results.

    Ask students to recall how what happens to the paper strip is like what happens when plant roots touch water in the soil. *(The roots take water from the dirt up into the plant.)*

4. Students staple one used strip of paper to their record sheets and write or dictate a sentence about what happened. Place completed forms in students' logbooks.

page 33

Roots Store Food

page 34

• Bring in a collection of vegetables, including various kinds of root vegetables—beets, carrots, radishes, turnips, rutabagas, jicama, etc. Explain that plants store extra food in their roots, and then have students determine which of the vegetables are roots.

• Some animals and people eat certain plant roots. Ask students to think about roots they may have eaten.

• Using page 34, students color the roots that people eat and cross out the roots people don't eat.

• Read and discuss the folded book on page 35 to reinforce the idea that all kinds of plants have roots and that roots have an important job to do for the plant.

Ask students to recall what jobs the roots do *(collect water for the plant, help hold the plant in the soil, store food).*

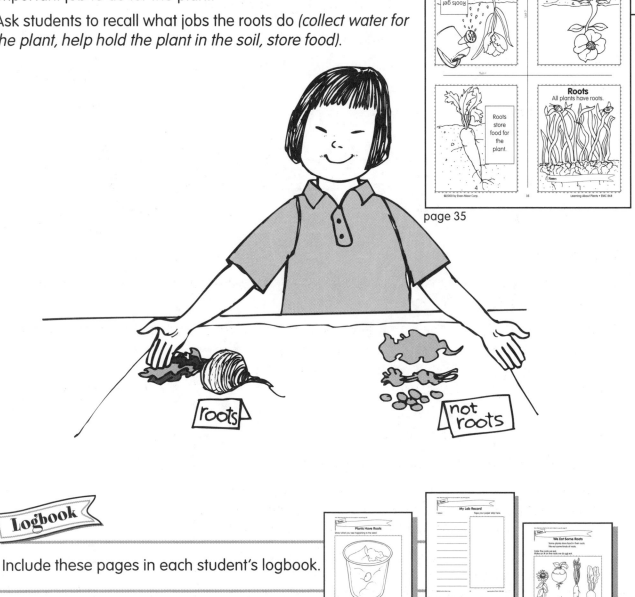

page 35

Logbook

Include these pages in each student's logbook.

Name

Plants Have Roots

Draw what you see happening to the seed.

Note: Reproduce this form for each student to use with page 30.

Name

My Lab Record

I saw:

Tape your paper strip here.

We Eat Some Roots

Some plants store food in their roots.

We eat some kinds of roots.

Color the roots we eat.
Make an **X** on the roots we do <u>not</u> eat.

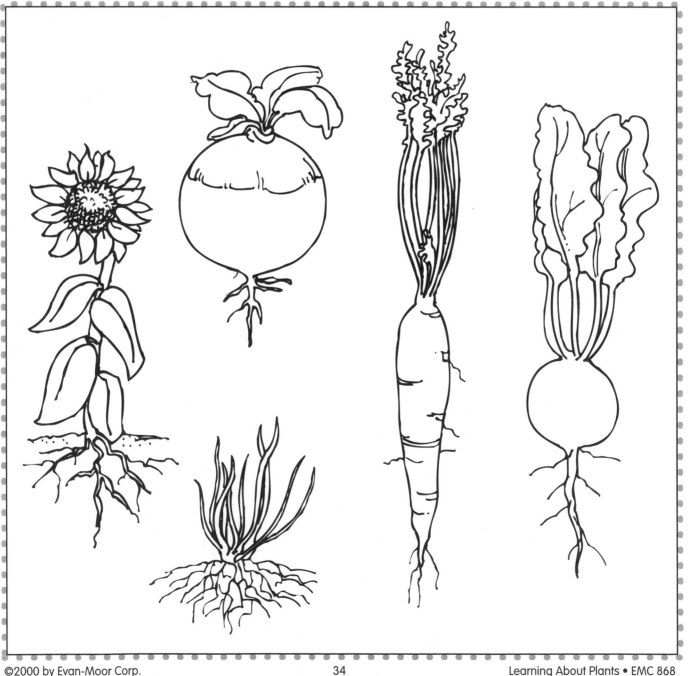

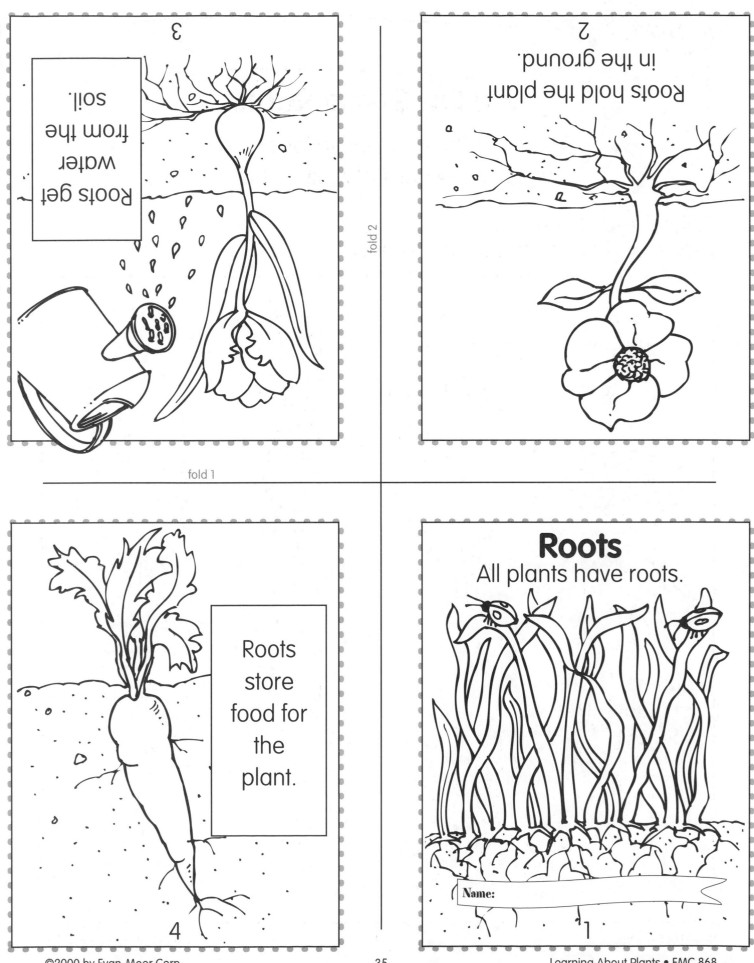

3

Roots get water from the soil.

fold 2

fold 1

2

Roots hold the plant in the ground.

4

Roots store food for the plant.

Roots
All plants have roots.

Name:

1

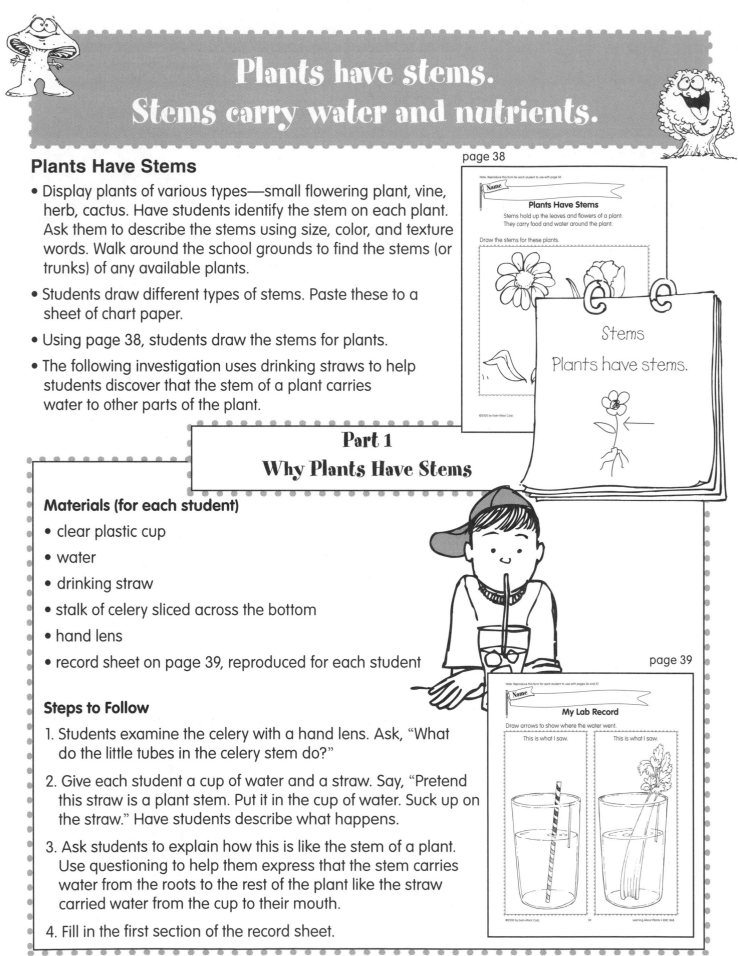

Plants have stems.
Stems carry water and nutrients.

Plants Have Stems

- Display plants of various types—small flowering plant, vine, herb, cactus. Have students identify the stem on each plant. Ask them to describe the stems using size, color, and texture words. Walk around the school grounds to find the stems (or trunks) of any available plants.

- Students draw different types of stems. Paste these to a sheet of chart paper.

- Using page 38, students draw the stems for plants.

- The following investigation uses drinking straws to help students discover that the stem of a plant carries water to other parts of the plant.

page 38

Plants Have Stems
Stems hold up the leaves and flowers of a plant.
They carry food and water around the plant.

Draw the stems for these plants.

Part 1
Why Plants Have Stems

Materials (for each student)

- clear plastic cup
- water
- drinking straw
- stalk of celery sliced across the bottom
- hand lens
- record sheet on page 39, reproduced for each student

page 39

My Lab Record
Draw arrows to show where the water went.
This is what I saw.   This is what I saw.

Steps to Follow

1. Students examine the celery with a hand lens. Ask, "What do the little tubes in the celery stem do?"

2. Give each student a cup of water and a straw. Say, "Pretend this straw is a plant stem. Put it in the cup of water. Suck up on the straw." Have students describe what happens.

3. Ask students to explain how this is like the stem of a plant. Use questioning to help them express that the stem carries water from the roots to the rest of the plant like the straw carried water from the cup to their mouth.

4. Fill in the first section of the record sheet.

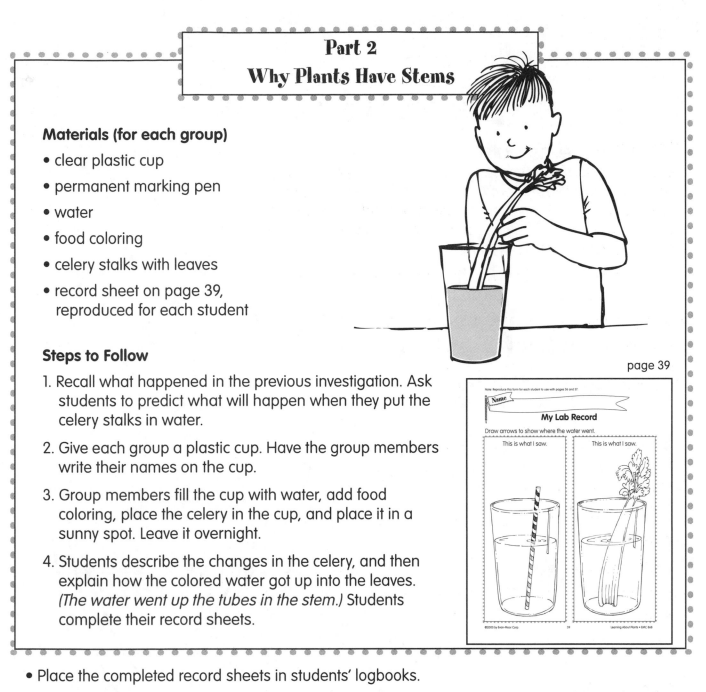

Part 2
Why Plants Have Stems

Materials (for each group)

• clear plastic cup

• permanent marking pen

• water

• food coloring

• celery stalks with leaves

• record sheet on page 39, reproduced for each student

Steps to Follow

1. Recall what happened in the previous investigation. Ask students to predict what will happen when they put the celery stalks in water.

2. Give each group a plastic cup. Have the group members write their names on the cup.

3. Group members fill the cup with water, add food coloring, place the celery in the cup, and place it in a sunny spot. Leave it overnight.

4. Students describe the changes in the celery, and then explain how the colored water got up into the leaves. *(The water went up the tubes in the stem.)* Students complete their record sheets.

page 39

• Place the completed record sheets in students' logbooks.

• Enjoy a snack of "stems" (celery) as you read and discuss the information in the minibook on pages 40–42.

Include these pages in each student's logbook.

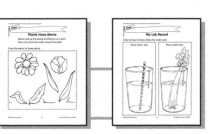

Name

Plants Have Stems

Stems hold up the leaves and flowers of a plant.
They carry food and water around the plant.

Draw the stems for these plants.

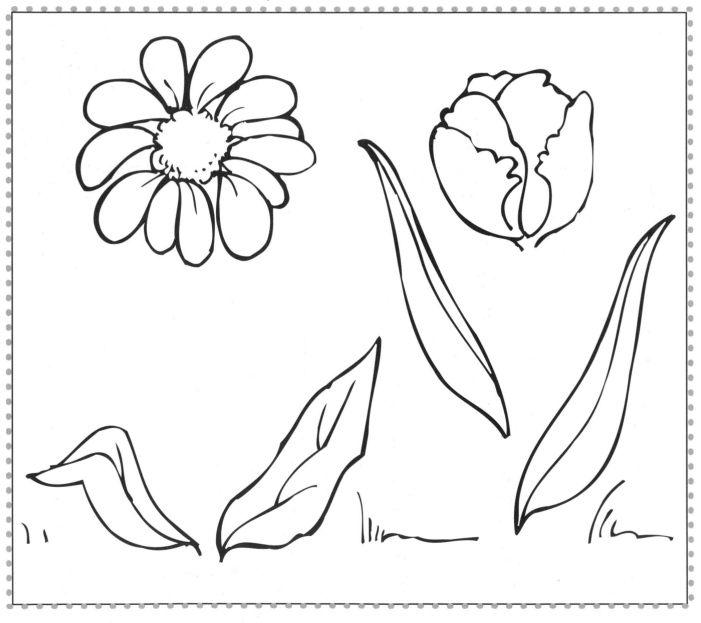

Note: Reproduce this form for each student to use with pages 36 and 37.

Name

My Lab Record

Draw arrows to show where the water went.

This is what I saw.

This is what I saw.

Learning About Plants • EMC 868

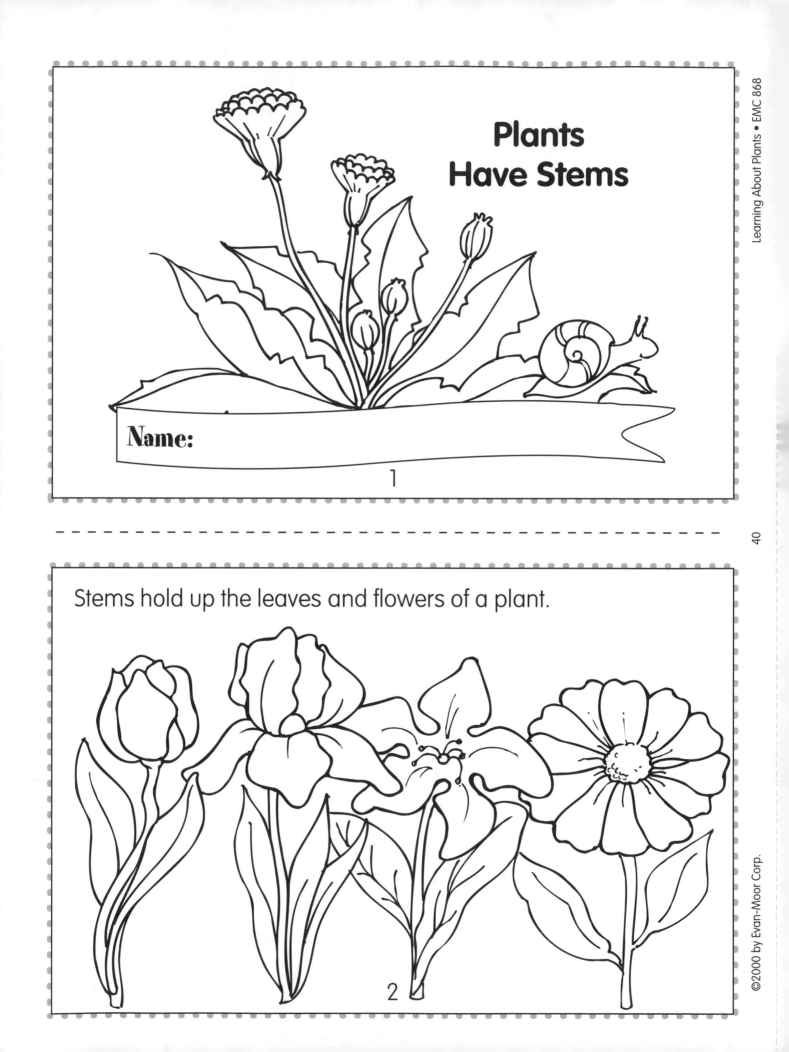

Plants
Have Stems

Name:

1

Stems hold up the leaves and flowers of a plant.

2

Trees have big, hard stems.
These stems are called trunks.

3

Learning About Plants • EMC 868

Most stems grow up.
Some grow along the ground.

4

Stems contain little tubes.
Tubes take water and
food around the
plant.

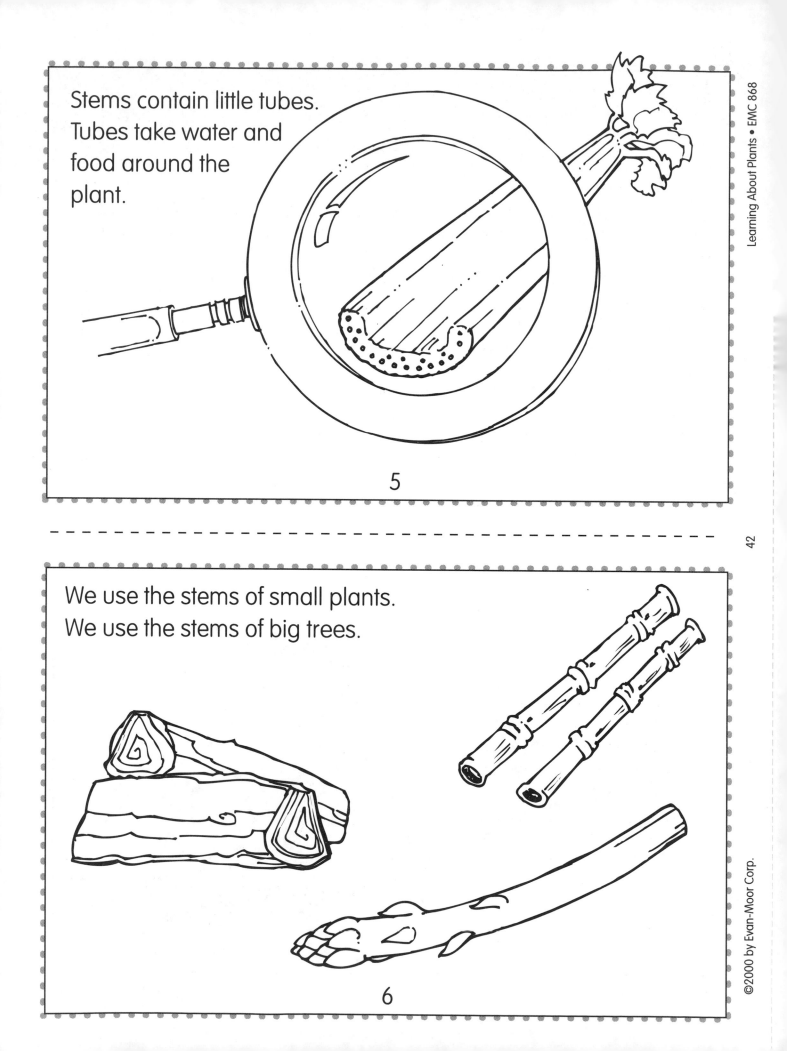

5

Learning About Plants • EMC 868

We use the stems of small plants.
We use the stems of big trees.

6

Plants have leaves.
Leaves make food.

Plants Have Leaves

- Bring in several plants with different kinds of leaves to share with students. Show the plants to students and ask them to describe the leaves on the plants. "How are they alike? How are they different?"

- Record student observations about leaves on a chart.

- Read *I Am a Leaf* by Jean Marzollo. Ask students to share what they recall from the story.

- Ask each student to bring three different leaves from home. Have additional leaves in class to guarantee variety and to provide for students who are unable to bring their own.

    Students examine the various shapes and leaf parts (midrib, veins). Ask them to speculate on the function of the ribs. Sort the leaves into categories by size, number of leaf parts, type of leaf (smooth, leathery, needles), and color.

- Students make leaf rubbings to put in their logbooks.

Leaves

Plants have leaves.
Some are big.
Some are little.
Leaves are green.

Leaf Rubbings

1. Place a leaf under a piece of paper. Rub across the leaf, using the side of a crayon.

2. Repeat with several different kinds of leaves.

3. Write "Leaves" across the paper. Optional: Add the name of the plant from which the leaf came.

Watch Leaves Grow

Provide opportunities for students to observe leaves growing.

• Plant lettuce seeds in a window box or large pot. Each day have students observe the lettuce. (Use a hand lens for a closer look at the new leaves.)

Ask students to describe the change that has taken place and to predict what the plant will look like the next day.

Select a student to illustrate the lettuce each day. Pin the pictures near the lettuce plants so students can see the progression of changes.

Harvest and nibble the leaves when they are large enough.

• Plant the tops of root vegetables (carrots, turnips, rutabagas, beets). Students will observe the growth of different types of leaves from these root vegetables.

Plant Root Tops

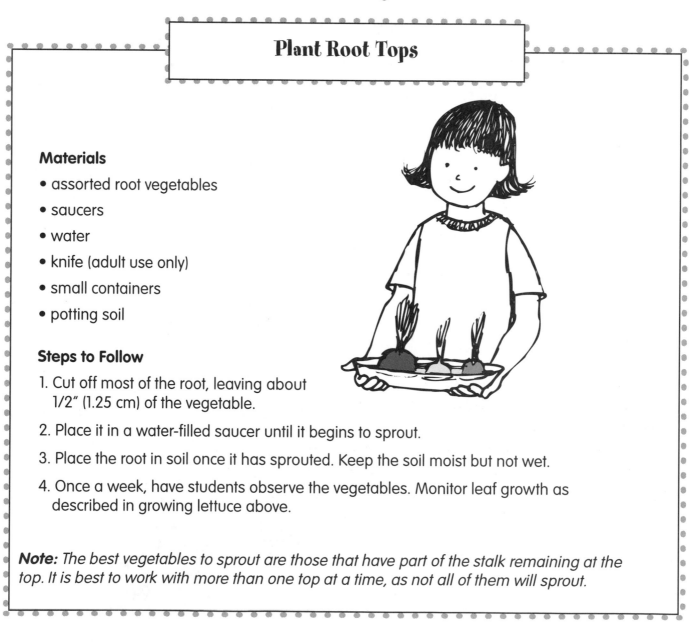

Materials

• assorted root vegetables

• saucers

• water

• knife (adult use only)

• small containers

• potting soil

Steps to Follow

1. Cut off most of the root, leaving about 1/2" (1.25 cm) of the vegetable.

2. Place it in a water-filled saucer until it begins to sprout.

3. Place the root in soil once it has sprouted. Keep the soil moist but not wet.

4. Once a week, have students observe the vegetables. Monitor leaf growth as described in growing lettuce above.

Note: The best vegetables to sprout are those that have part of the stalk remaining at the top. It is best to work with more than one top at a time, as not all of them will sprout.

A Leaf's Job

- Read *How Plants Get Food* by Meish Goldish to help students understand that green leaves are like food factories for the plant. Don't expect them to understand the process by which this occurs. At this point it is enough that they recognize that leaves are important to the life of a plant.

- Read and discuss the information in the minibook on pages 46–48.

- Ask students to recall why plants need leaves. Record their responses on a chart. Make corrections or additions as students acquire more information.

pages 46–48

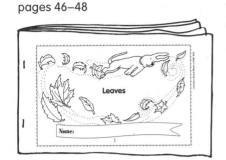

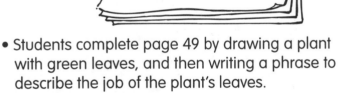

The Job of a Leaf
Leaves make food for the plant.

page 49

page 50

- Students complete page 49 by drawing a plant with green leaves, and then writing a phrase to describe the job of the plant's leaves.

Many Kinds of Leaves

- Provide samples or pictures of a pine bough, fir bough, cactus, etc. (things with needles). Have students describe what they see. Discuss that leaves may look different but have the same function. Ask students to recall that function *(to make food for the plant)*.

- Read *It Could Still Be a Leaf* by Allan Fowler to expand students' understanding of the variety of leaf forms.

- Students complete the activity on page 50 to show what they have learned about leaves.

Logbook

Include these pages in each student's logbook.

Learning About Plants • EMC 868

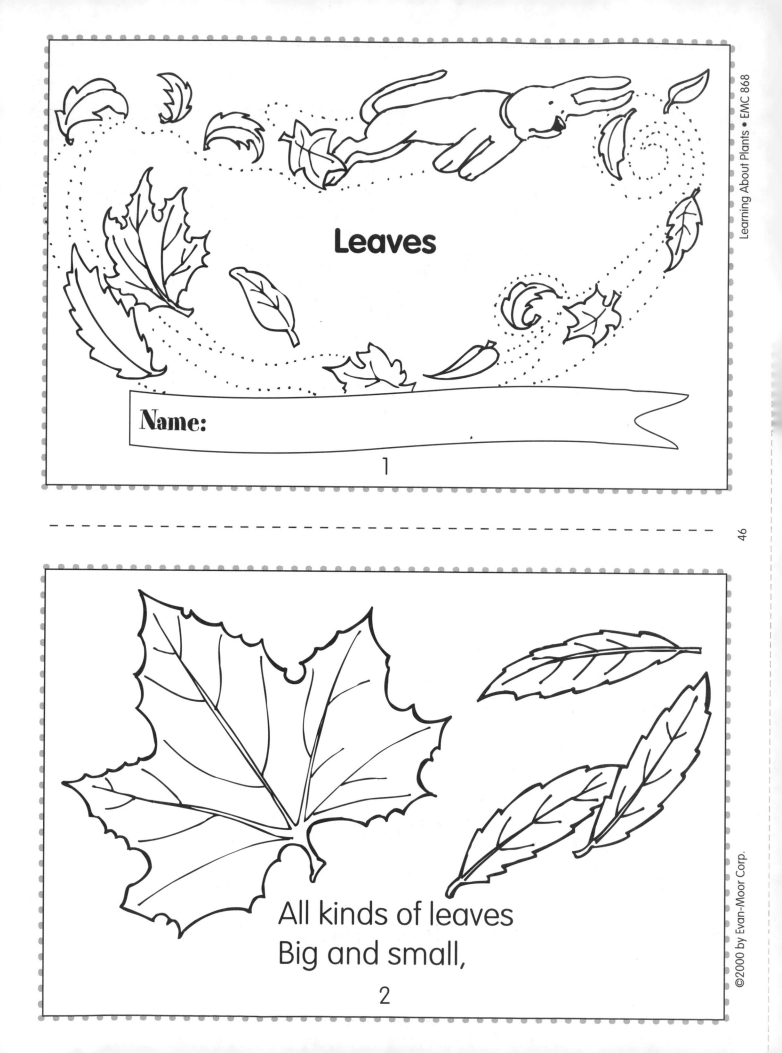

Leaves

Name:

1

Learning About Plants • EMC 868

All kinds of leaves
Big and small,

2

One leaf or many,

3

On plants short and tall.

4

Animals eat leaves
from a bush or a tree.

5

And leaves can be
food for you and
for me.

6

Name

The Job of a Leaf

Draw a plant with green leaves.

The job of a leaf is _____.

Note: Reproduce this form for each student to use with page 45.

Name

Plants Have Leaves

Color the leaves green.

Make an **X** on the leaves that are called **needles**.

Some plants have flowers.
Flowers make seeds.

Some Plants Have Flowers

- Bring in a large mixed bouquet of common flowers. Ask, "What do we call the things in this bouquet?" *(flowers)* Have students describe the various flowers by size, color, and smell. Ask them to name the different varieties. Provide any names they don't know.

- Divide the class into small groups. Give each group several different types of flowers and a hand lens. Allow time for students to look more closely at their flowers. (Answer any questions in a simple, but accurate manner. This is an opportunity to observe that while flowers are different, they share some common elements [petals, pollen, etc.].)

  Have books such as *Usborne First Nature Flowers* by Rosamund K. Cox and Barbara Cork available as other sources illustrating flowering plants.

- Provide time for students to share their observations with the class. Write their responses on a chart.

- Using page 54, students color the flowers.

- Paint a spring flower garden on the windows in your classroom. Add a *small amount* of liquid soap to the tempera to make final cleanup easier. Or, have students paint flowers on paper and bind them in a cover to create a book.

page 54

Learning About Plants • EMC 868

Flowers Make Seeds

- Students color the seeds in the plants on page 55.

- Read and discuss the minibook on pages 56 and 57 and appropriate pages from *The Reason for a Flower* by Ruth Heller to introduce the idea that flowers make seeds. Add this new information to the chart entitled "Flowers."

There are Many Kinds of Seeds

- Show students a coconut and some sunflower seeds and ask, "What part of a plant are these?" Use the extreme difference in size to motivate a discussion about how seeds are different.

- Begin a seed collection in your classroom. Gather seeds from neighborhood plants, the supermarket (dry seeds—popcorn, dried beans; fresh seeds—corn in husks, peas in pods, apples), students' lunch boxes, and nearby vacant lots or fields.

Sort the seeds in various ways:
    size (in size order)
    color (black, white, brown)
    shape (oval/round, smooth/bumpy, sphere/flat)
    weight (large seeds such as coconut, avocado,
           peach; small seeds such as apple, orange,
           pumpkin)

Glue the seeds to a chart for the class logbook, tape them into scrapbooks, or display them on a table.

page 55

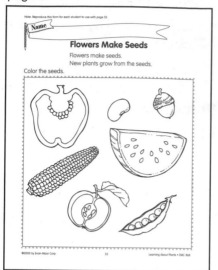

pages 56 and 57

Flowers Need Pollen

- Read *Flower, Why Do You Smell So Nice?* by Francesca Grazzini to begin a discussion of how flowers attract insects and birds by their scent or color.

  Ask students to recall what they learned from the story. Add the new information to the class "Flower" logbook page. (At this level students only need to know that flowers need pollen to make seeds.)

- Play the "Bee to Flower" game described below.

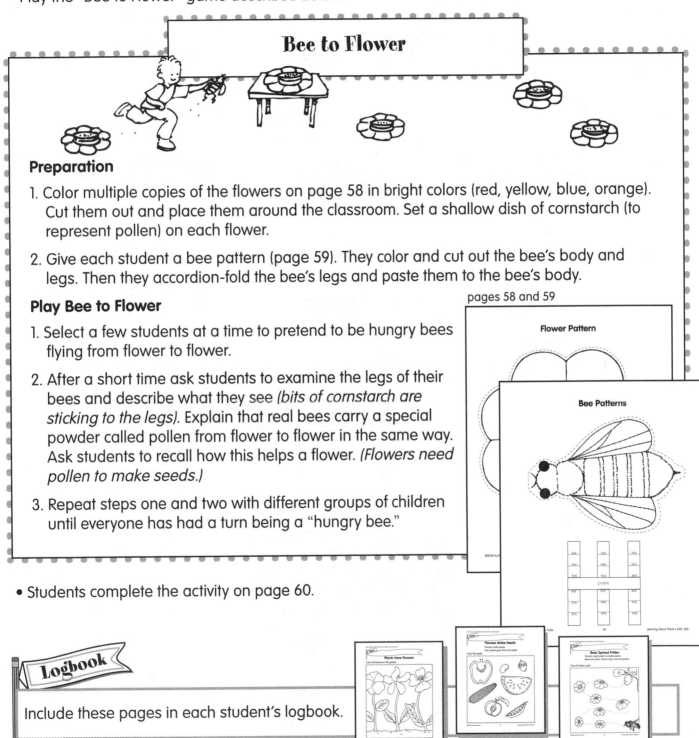

Bee to Flower

Preparation

1. Color multiple copies of the flowers on page 58 in bright colors (red, yellow, blue, orange). Cut them out and place them around the classroom. Set a shallow dish of cornstarch (to represent pollen) on each flower.

2. Give each student a bee pattern (page 59). They color and cut out the bee's body and legs. Then they accordion-fold the bee's legs and paste them to the bee's body.

Play Bee to Flower

1. Select a few students at a time to pretend to be hungry bees flying from flower to flower.

2. After a short time ask students to examine the legs of their bees and describe what they see *(bits of cornstarch are sticking to the legs)*. Explain that real bees carry a special powder called pollen from flower to flower in the same way. Ask students to recall how this helps a flower. *(Flowers need pollen to make seeds.)*

3. Repeat steps one and two with different groups of children until everyone has had a turn being a "hungry bee."

pages 58 and 59

Flower Pattern

Bee Patterns

- Students complete the activity on page 60.

Logbook

Include these pages in each student's logbook.

Name

Plants Have Flowers

Color the flowers in this garden.

Note: Reproduce this form for each student to use with page 52.

Name

Flowers Make Seeds

Flowers make seeds.

New plants grow from the seeds.

Color the seeds.

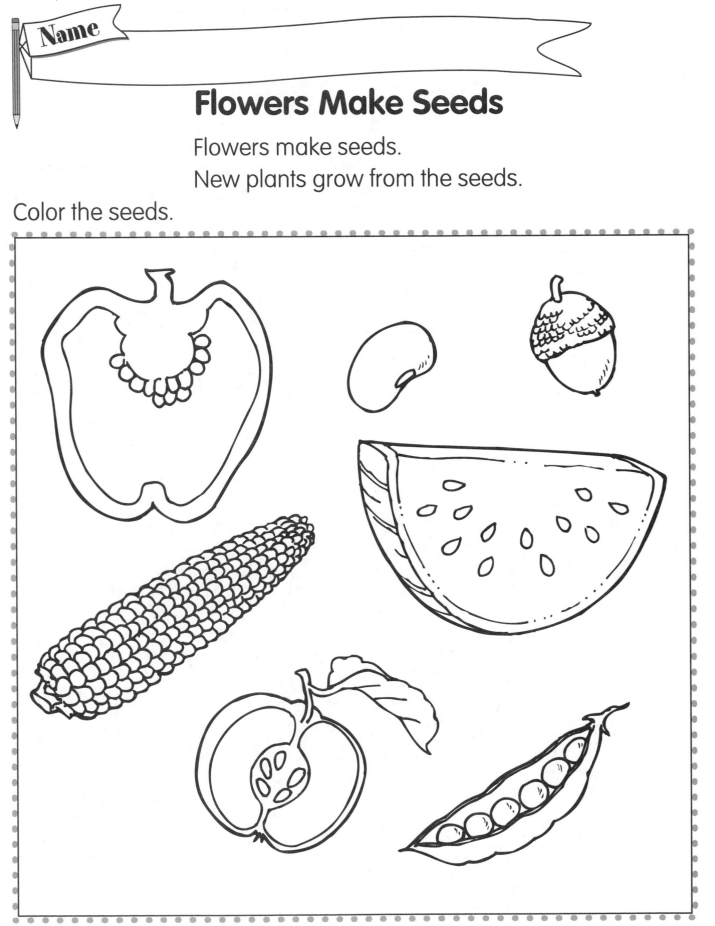

Flowers

Name: _____

1

Learning About Plants • EMC 868

small flowers

big flowers

2

colorful flowers

3

All these flowers have one job.
They make seeds.

4

Flower Pattern

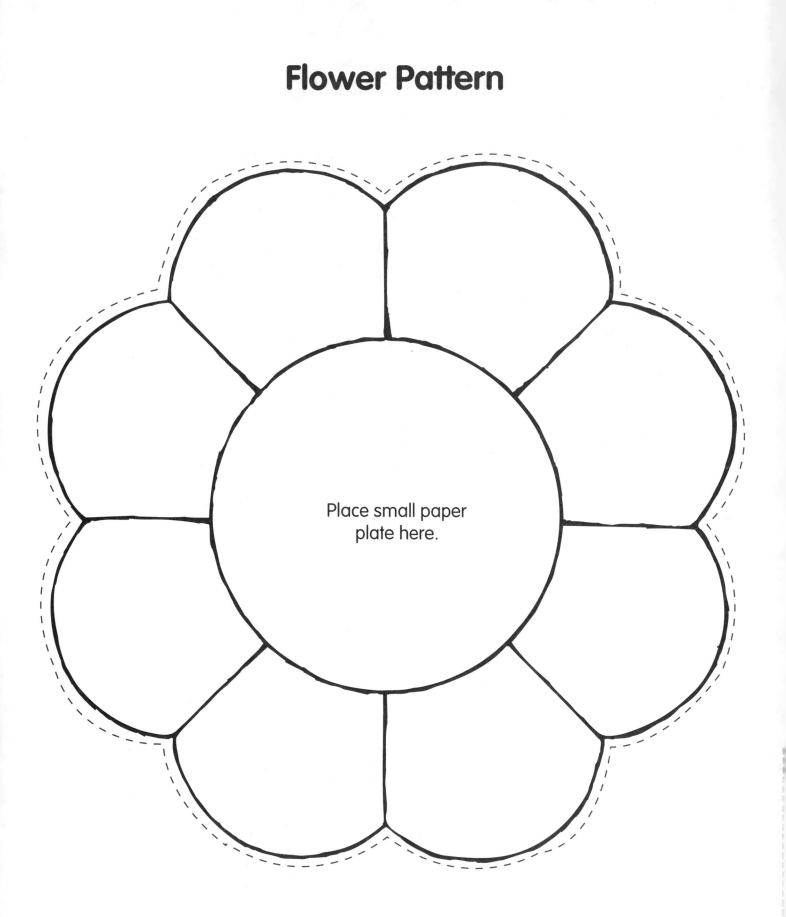

Place small paper plate here.

Learning About Plants • EMC 868

Bee Patterns

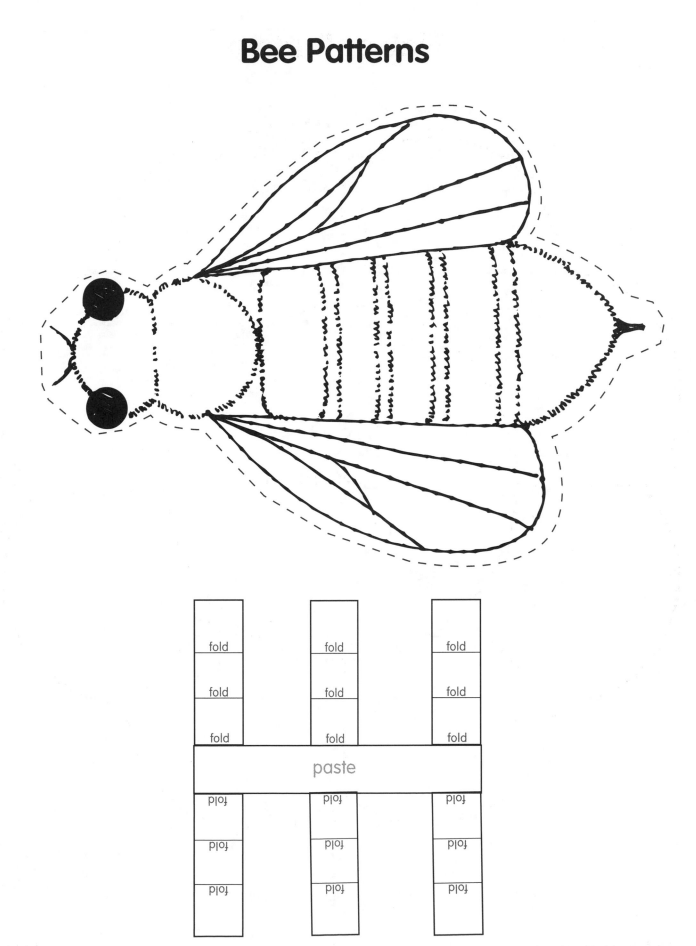

Learning About Plants • EMC 868

Name

Bees Spread Pollen

Flowers need pollen to make seeds.
Bees and other insects help move the pollen.

Trace the bee's path.

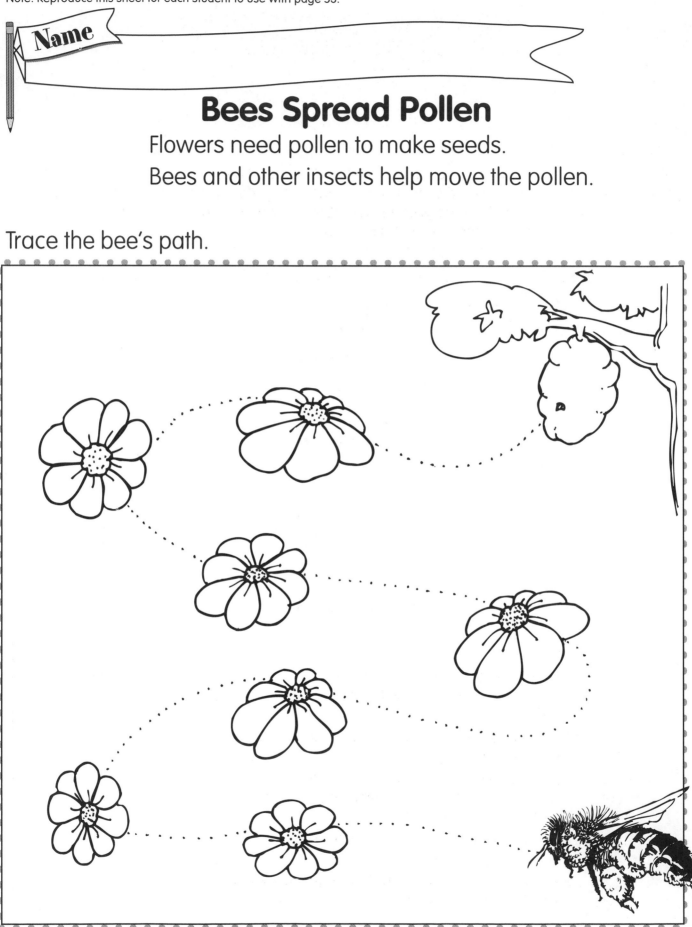

Seeds grow into new plants.

The Job of a Seed

Show some seeds from the class collection. Explain that while seeds may look different and come from different plants, they are the same in an important way. Ask students to tell you in what way they are the same. Record their ideas on the chalkboard, and then do the investigation below to observe what happens to a seed when it is planted.

Seeds Grow into New Plants

Materials
(for each student)

- plastic cup

- lima beans or peas (soak overnight)

- permanent marking pen

- record sheet on page 63, reproduced for each student

(for work area)

- potting soil

- pail and scoop

- newspapers

- water

Getting Ready

Cover the work area with newspapers to make cleanup easier. Put potting soil in a large plastic container along with a scoop or large spoon. Designate a place where the plants will be kept as they grow.

Steps to Follow

1. Students write their names on their plastic cups, then follow these steps:

   a. Fill the cup with potting soil.

   b. Plant three lima beans in the cup. Place the beans near the sides so the roots, stems, and leaves can be seen as they begin to grow.

   c. Water the plant and set it in a sunny spot. Keep the soil damp but not wet.

2. Every day or so have students observe their plants to see what is happening. Have them share what they see and then record it on their record sheets.

3. When the plants have several leaves, send them home to be planted in pots or gardens.

4. Review what students observed as they watched their seeds sprout and grow. Record this on a chart.

page 63

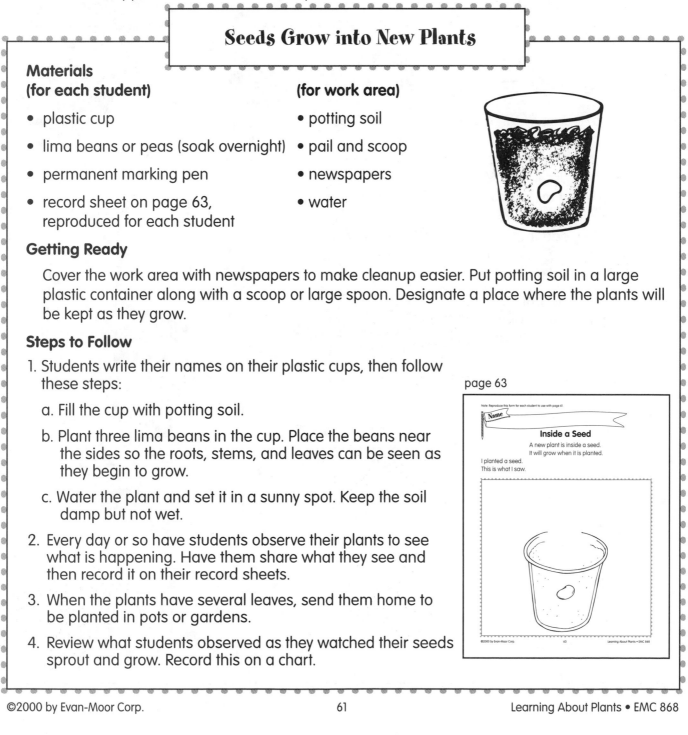

Note: Reproduce this form for each student to use with page 61.

Name

Inside a Seed

A new plant is inside a seed.
It will grow when it is planted.

I planted a seed.
This is what I saw.

©2000 by Evan-Moor Corp.　　63　　Learning About Plants • EMC 868

More About Seeds

- Read and discuss the minibook on pages 64 and 65. Then make any additions or corrections to the information about seeds in the class logbook.

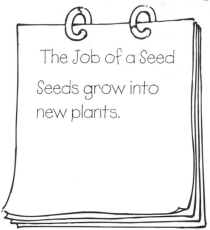

The Job of a Seed
Seeds grow into new plants.

pages 64 and 65

- Read *I'm a Seed* by Jean Marzollo about a seed that doesn't know what kind it is. Extend learning by showing sunflower seeds and asking, "What kind of seeds are these? What kind of plant will a sunflower seed grow into?" Repeat with several common kinds of seeds (apple, orange, corn, pea, etc.). Help students verbalize the idea that a seed will grow into the same kind of plant it came from. Add the statement to "The Job of a Seed" chart.

- Provide each student with the following seeds—sunflower, corn, pumpkin, and bean. Have them identify each seed and then paste it in the correct box on the record sheet on page 66.

page 66

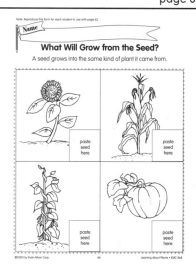

Include these pages in each student's logbook.

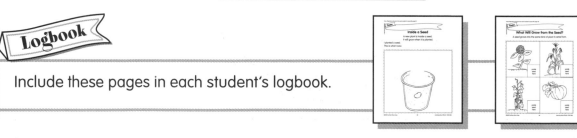

Name

Inside a Seed

A new plant is inside a seed.
It will grow when it is planted.

I planted a seed.
This is what I saw.

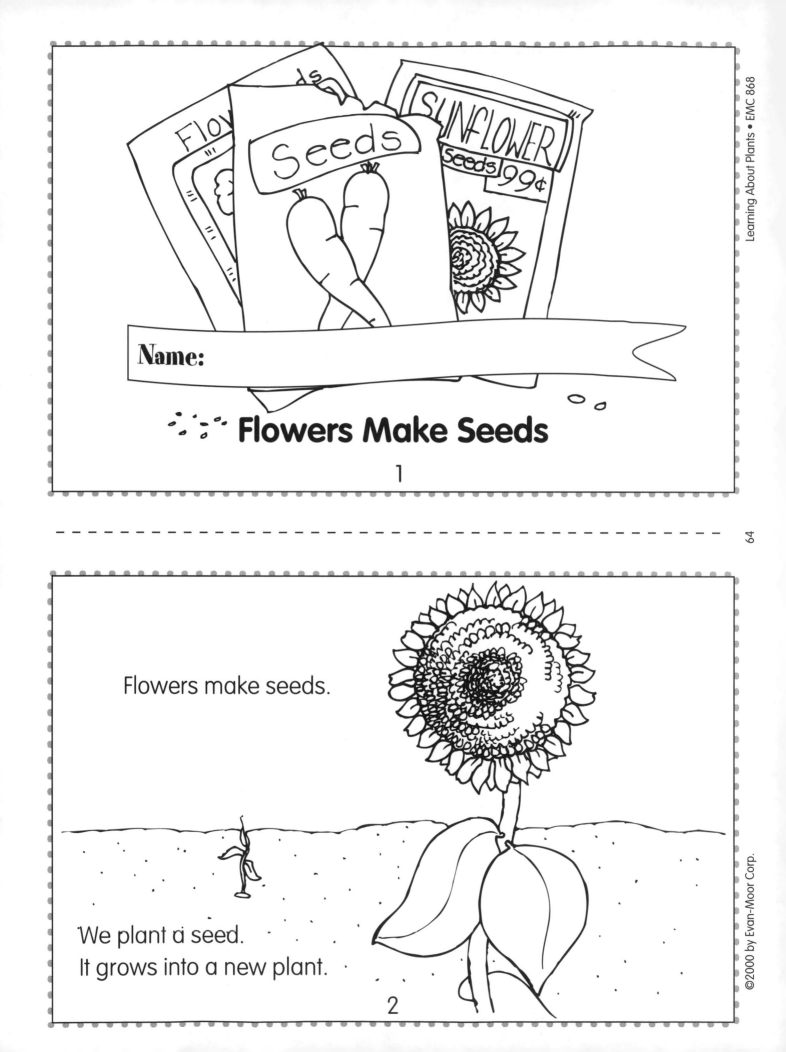

Name:

Flowers Make Seeds

1

Flowers make seeds.

We plant a seed.
It grows into a new plant.

2

Tomato seeds grow into tomato plants.

Bean seeds grow into bean plants.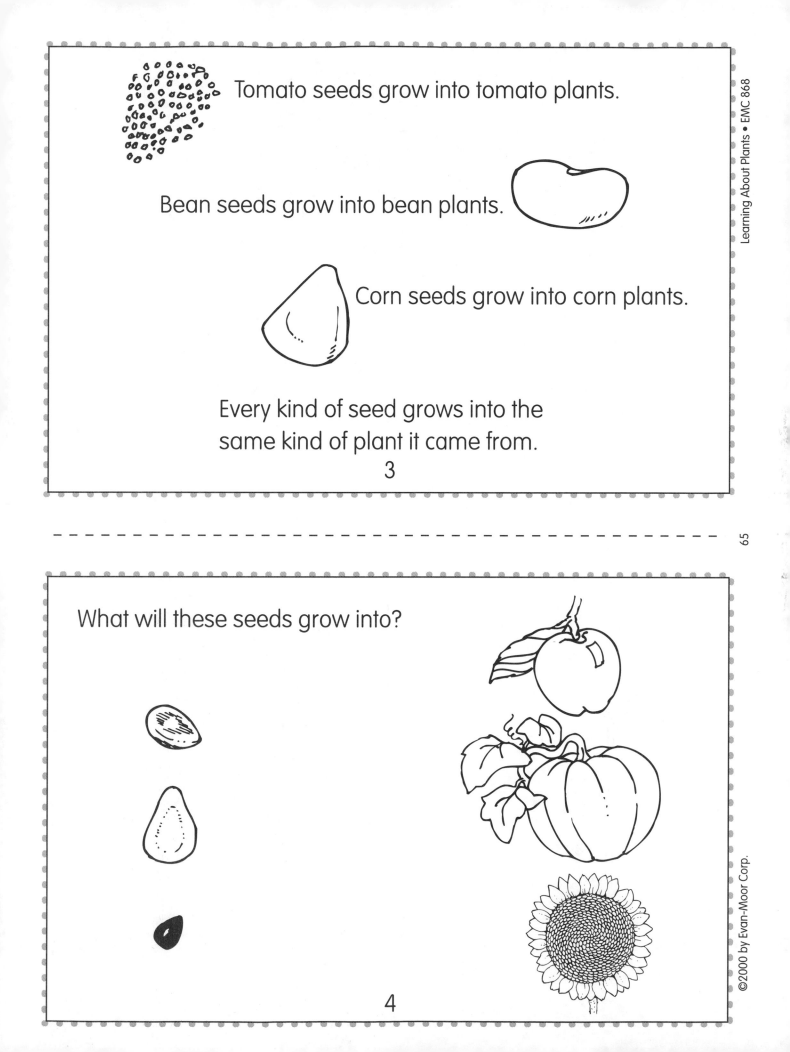

Corn seeds grow into corn plants.

Every kind of seed grows into the
same kind of plant it came from.

3

Learning About Plants • EMC 868

What will these seeds grow into?

4

Note: Reproduce this form for each student to use with page 62.

What Will Grow from the Seed?

A seed grows into the same kind of plant it came from.

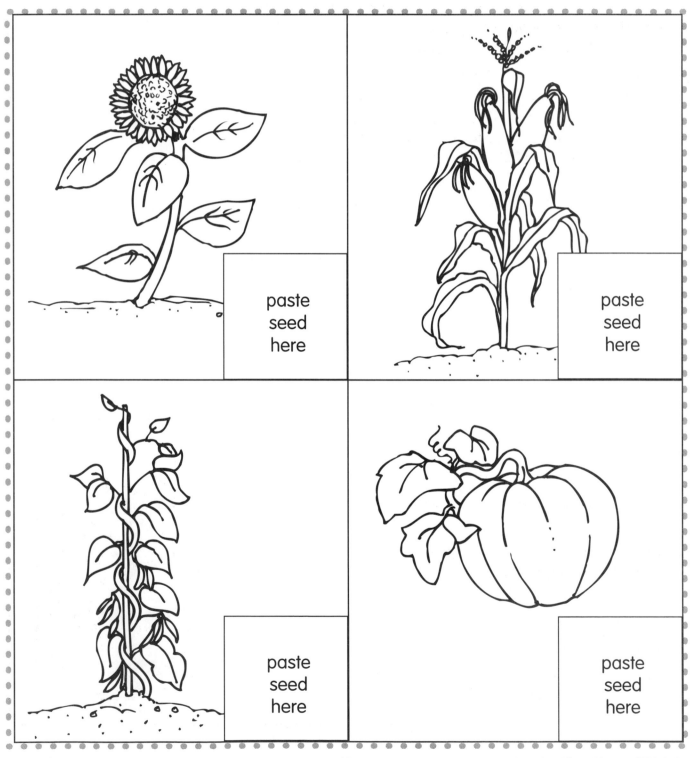

paste
seed
here

paste
seed
here

paste
seed
here

paste
seed
here

 Learning About Plants • EMC 868

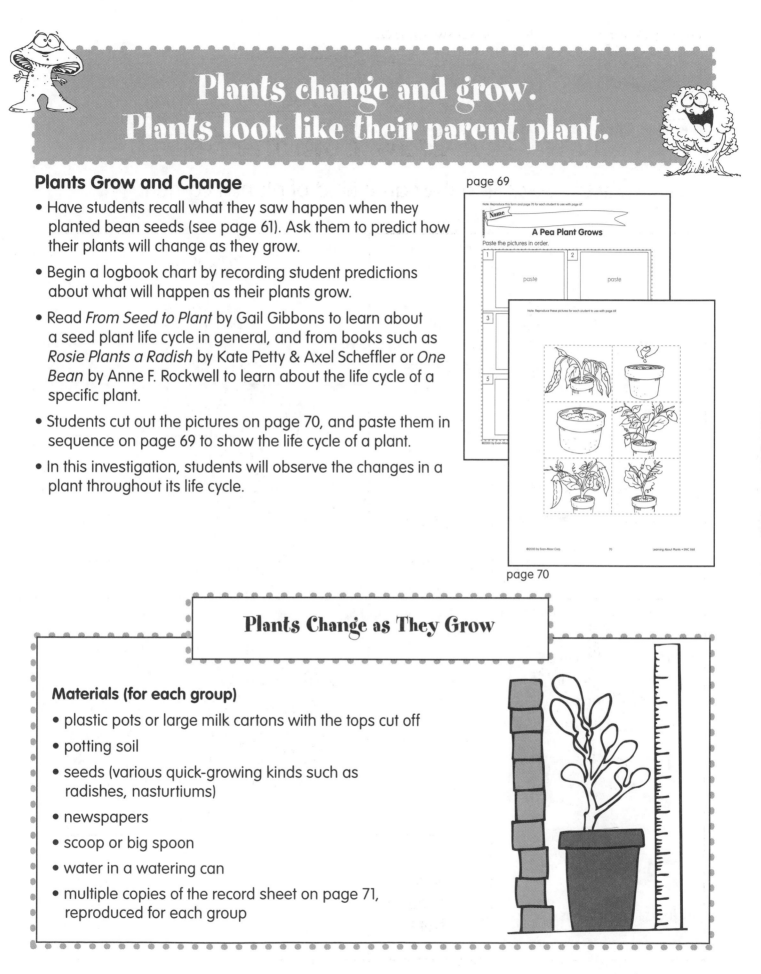

Plants change and grow.
Plants look like their parent plant.

Plants Grow and Change

- Have students recall what they saw happen when they planted bean seeds (see page 61). Ask them to predict how their plants will change as they grow.

- Begin a logbook chart by recording student predictions about what will happen as their plants grow.

- Read *From Seed to Plant* by Gail Gibbons to learn about a seed plant life cycle in general, and from books such as *Rosie Plants a Radish* by Kate Petty & Axel Scheffler or *One Bean* by Anne F. Rockwell to learn about the life cycle of a specific plant.

- Students cut out the pictures on page 70, and paste them in sequence on page 69 to show the life cycle of a plant.

- In this investigation, students will observe the changes in a plant throughout its life cycle.

page 69

A Pea Plant Grows
Paste the pictures in order.

page 70

Plants Change as They Grow

Materials (for each group)

- plastic pots or large milk cartons with the tops cut off
- potting soil
- seeds (various quick-growing kinds such as radishes, nasturtiums)
- newspapers
- scoop or big spoon
- water in a watering can
- multiple copies of the record sheet on page 71, reproduced for each group

Steps to Follow

1. Cover the work area with newspapers. Put potting soil into a large plastic container along with a scoop. Divide the class into small groups. Give each group a pot and seeds.

2. Call groups up one at a time to plant their seeds.

   a. Students in the group write their names on the pot.

   b. Fill the pot with soil and plant several seeds. Water carefully so the seeds are not disturbed.

   c. Place the pot in a sunny spot. Water as needed.

   d. Post the record sheet by the plant. Keep a weekly record of the plant's progress, recording growth in height and other observable changes.

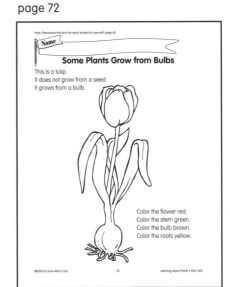

page 71

Plants from Bulbs

• Ask students to recall what they did to grow a new plant. *(We planted seeds.)*

Show a plant that grows from a bulb. Ask, "What would I plant to grow this kind of flower?" Explain that not all plants grow from seeds. Remove the plant from the soil and show the bulb.

• Then read appropriate parts of *Bulb to Tulip* by Oliver S. Owen. Discuss how these plants grow without seeds.

• Students then complete page 72 for their logbooks.

Making Connections

Review how plants change as they grow. Ask students to share ways people change as they grow older.

page 72

Include these pages in each student's logbook.

Name

A Pea Plant Grows

Paste the pictures in order.

1	2
paste	paste

3	4
paste	paste

5	6
paste	paste

Learning About Plants • EMC 868

Note: Reproduce these pictures for each student to use with page 69.

Our Plant Record

We planted _____ seeds.

Today it looks like this:

paste a seed
here

Our Group:

_____

_____

_____

_____

Date:

_____

It is _____ tall.

Name

Some Plants Grow from Bulbs

This is a tulip.
It does not grow from a seed.
It grows from a bulb.

Color the flower red.
Color the stem green.
Color the bulb brown.
Color the roots yellow.

A plant needs air, water, food, and light.

What Plants Need

- Ask students to think of places where they have seen plants growing. *(My grandma grows vegetables in her garden. We have plants in our house. There are flowers growing in front of the school.)* Then ask them to describe how the plants are cared for. *(Grandma waters her plants. My dad puts plant food on the plants. Mom says her plants need to sit where they can get sunshine.)*

  Show students a healthy-looking plant and one that is almost dead. Ask, "Which plant is healthy? How can you tell? What do you think happened to the other plant?"

- Record student responses on a chart entitled "Plants need…." You will be adding to and revising the chart as students do the following investigations.

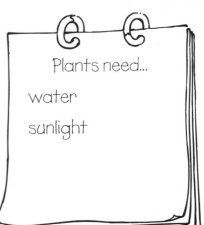

Plants need…

water

sunlight

Plants Need Sunlight

Explain to students that they will be watching two plants to see what happens when one gets light and one does not.

Materials

- 2 small green plants
- a brown paper bag
- record sheet on page 75, reproduced for each student

Steps to Follow

1. Put two plants in a sunny window, covering one with a paper bag. Ask students to predict what will happen to the two plants.

2. Water both plants as needed, but always keep the one plant covered.

3. Watch what happens over the next few weeks. Each time the plants are examined, have students describe what they see.

4. At the end of the investigation, point to the unhealthy plant and ask, "What happened to this plant? Why does it look so bad?" *(It didn't get any sunlight. Plants need sunlight.)*

5. Help students complete the record sheet for the investigation.

page 75

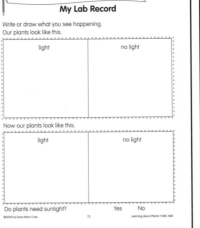

Learning About Plants • EMC 868

Plants Need Water

Explain to students that they will be watching two plants to see what happens when one gets water and one does not.

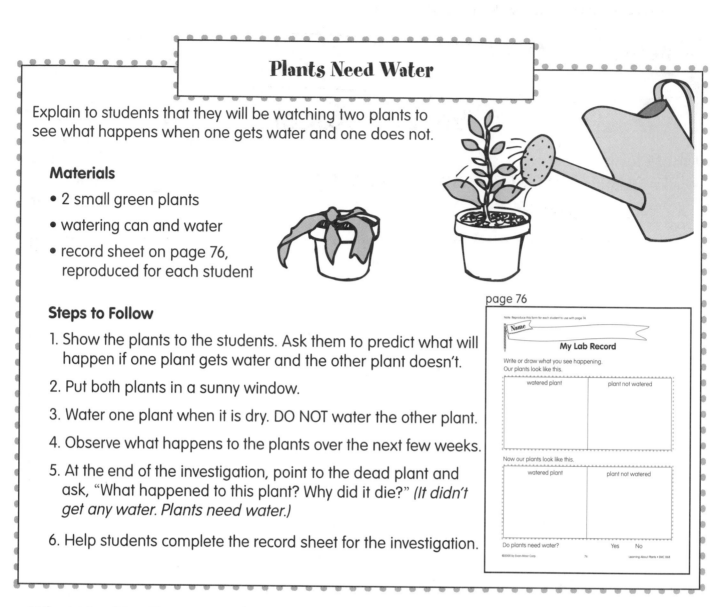

Materials

- 2 small green plants
- watering can and water
- record sheet on page 76, reproduced for each student

Steps to Follow

1. Show the plants to the students. Ask them to predict what will happen if one plant gets water and the other plant doesn't.

2. Put both plants in a sunny window.

3. Water one plant when it is dry. DO NOT water the other plant.

4. Observe what happens to the plants over the next few weeks.

5. At the end of the investigation, point to the dead plant and ask, "What happened to this plant? Why did it die?" *(It didn't get any water. Plants need water.)*

6. Help students complete the record sheet for the investigation.

page 76

What Healthy Plants Need

page 77

- Read appropriate parts of *How Plants Get Food* by Meish Goldish, *What Makes a Flower Grow?* by Susan Mayes, and/or *Dandelion Adventures* by L. Patricia Kite. Ask students to recall what the plants needed in order to grow. Make changes and additions to the class chart "Plants need…."

- Using page 77, students add sunlight and water to illustrate what a green plant needs in order to grow.

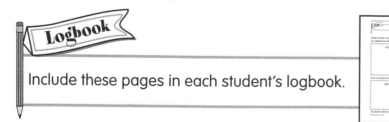

Include these pages in each student's logbook.

Name

My Lab Record

Write or draw what you see happening.

Our plants look like this.

light	no light

Now our plants look like this.

light	no light

Do plants need sunlight?   Yes   No

Name

My Lab Record

Write or draw what you see happening.
Our plants look like this.

watered plant	plant not watered

Now our plants look like this.

watered plant	plant not watered

Do plants need water?   Yes   No

Name

What Do Plants Need?

Plants need sunlight.
Plants need water.
Plants use them to make food.

Draw a sun in the sky.
Draw water from the hose to the plants.

Animals and people need plants.

Animals Need Plants

- Brainstorm to list the ways animals use plants *(for food, as a place to live)*.

- Each student paints a picture of one animal showing how it uses plants. Pin these to a bulletin board entitled "Animals Need Plants."

People Need Plants

- Recall the ways animals use plants. Then ask, "Why do people need plants?" Record student responses on a chart.

- Bring in a basket of plant products from the supermarket. Try to include something for each part of the plant that people eat. Ask students to identify the food and name the part of the plant it comes from.

  Prepare a plate of samples to nibble.

  Note: *Be aware of any food allergies your students might have before doing any of the tasting-day activities in this book. Remind students that they should only eat plant parts they know are food. Not every plant is edible.*

People Need Plants

We eat plants.

We get wood from plants.

- Read the folded book on page 79 together and discuss ways people use plants.

  Have students identify things in the classroom that are made from plants. Things made from wood will be easiest for them to identify. Point out other ways we use plants such as paper made from trees and some of the clothing we wear (cotton, linen).

- Using page 80, students match each plant to the way it is used by people.

pages 79 and 80

We Use Plants

Include this page in each student's logbook.

People eat plants.
People build furniture
and houses from trees.

3

Animals eat plants.
Some animals eat trees.

2

fold 2

fold 1

People make clothes from
parts of some plants.

4

**Animals
and
People
Need Plants**

1

Name

We Use Plants

Match.

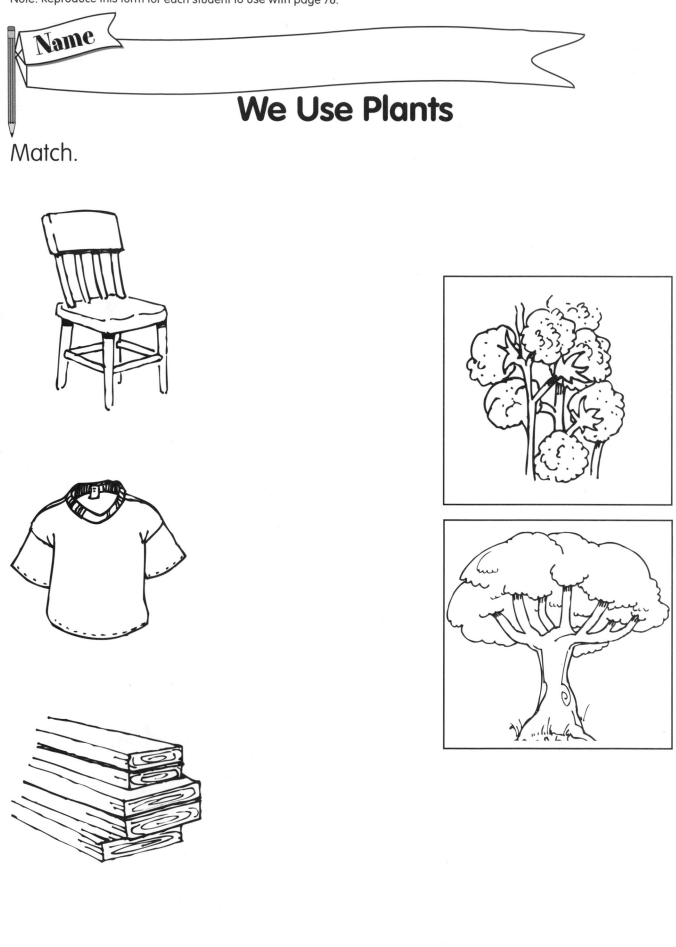